Copyright © 2018 LoveBook® LLC
Cover and Internal Design © 2018 LoveBook® LLC
Puns puntificated & punctuated by Rob Patterson
Design & Illustrations by Brendan Maidment,
Heather Coutteau; First Edition

All rights reserved.

Published by Neuron Publishing
www.neuronpublishing.com
www.LoveBookOnline.com

This book was inspired
by two friends hanging out,
paying com-pun-ments
to a 'total babe'.

if you
were a children's
playground
game you'd be
hot-scotch

If you were a tropical fruit

you'd be a

i like you a whole latte!

if you were a resturant side item

you'd be french-wise

You sure are a-peel-ing

if you were a piece of jewelry you would be allure-ring

IF YOU ONLY
HAD ONE HAND

IF YOU JUST
CAME OFF THE GRILL
YOU WOULD BE
BARBE-CUTE

IF YOU WERE A MUSICAL INSTUMENT YOU'D BE A CHARM-ONICA!

if you were a type of explosive you'd be

if you
were a season
you'd be
HAWT-UMN

IF YOU WERE TO ENFORCE THE LAW YOU'D BE A DEP-BEAUTY

IF YOU WERE A DAIRY PRODUCT

YOU'D BE HOT-TAGE CHEESE

even if you couldn't read...

you'd still be illiter-great!

KANYE FEEL THE LOVE?!

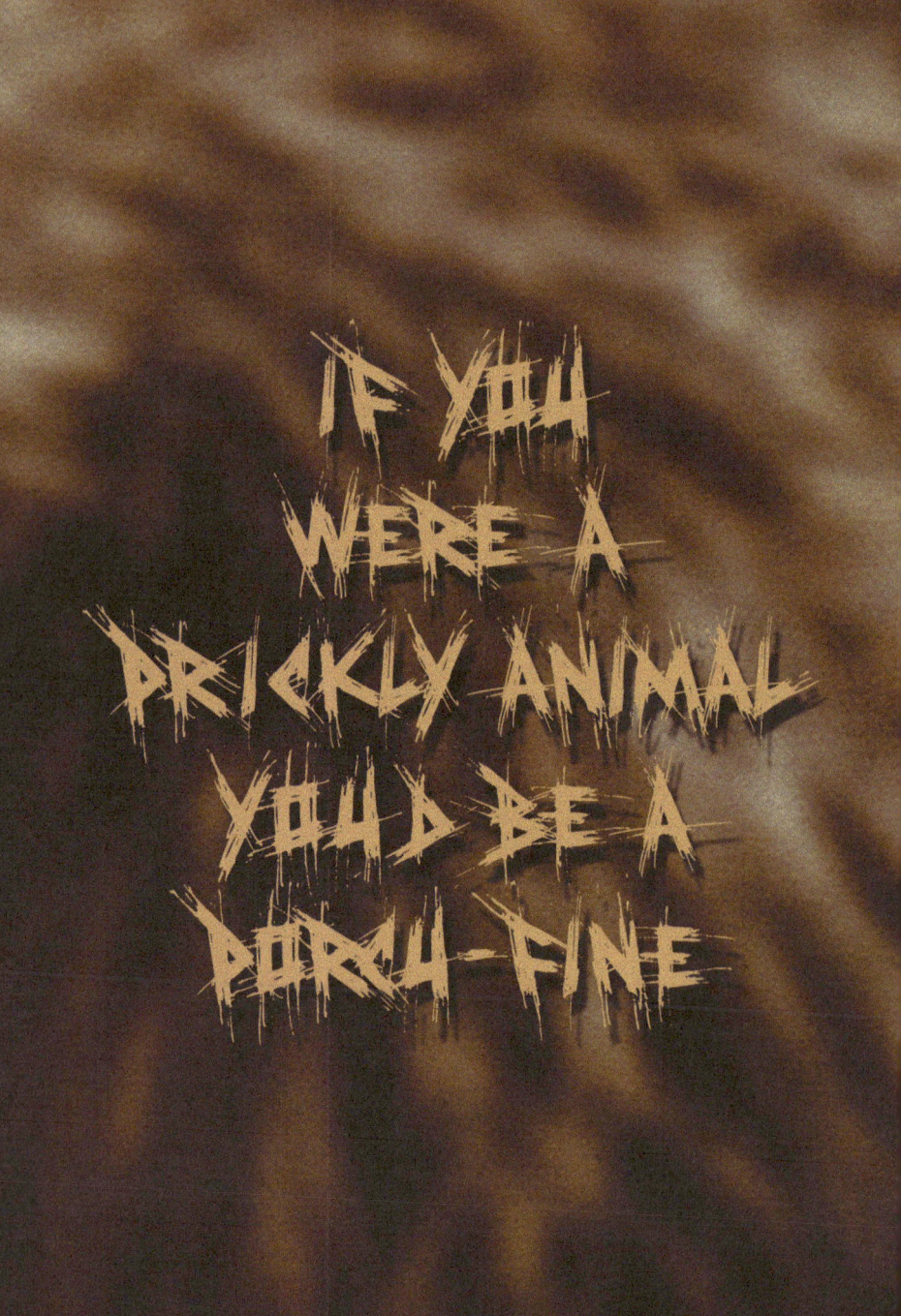

WE SURE MAKE A — A — GREAT PEAR!

OOPS... I MEAN WE SURE MAKE A GREAT PAIR!

IF
YOU WERE
EVERYONE'S
FAVORITE
SANDWICH
SPREAD...

YOU'D BE HOTTELLA!

My Heart "Beets" for You!

IF YOU WERE TO
WIN AN AWARD

IT WOULD BE FOR
SMART-ICIPATION!

IF YOU WERE A COOKIE

You're such a
cutie pie!

I LOVE YOU TO THE CORE

if you were lip moisturizer

**IF YOU WERE
A DOG YOU'D
BE A 'HOT'WEILER**

we
are
like
two
G's
in a
pod

if you got paid to kill people who had committed crimes

you would be an exe-cute-tioner

YOU'D BE A FINECONE

You are boo-tiful

If you were a communication device

if you were a flying insect
you'd of course be a
beaut-erfly

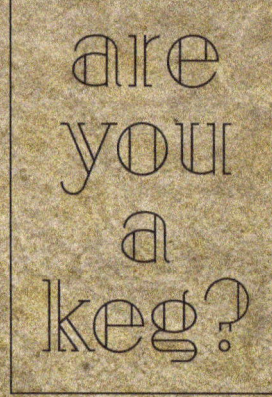

WE
WERE
MINT
TO BE

you are bee-utiful

if you were an illegal substance, you'd be a narc-hotic

if you were a reproductive organ, you'd be a...

If you were an alcoholic beverage

IF YOU WERE A TRANSFORMER YOU WOULD BE OPTIMUS-FINE

if you were a sport

I
love
your
doggy
style

Thanks for pudding up with me

YOU SURE ARE
TEA-RIFFIC

if you were a jazz instrument

i love you

from my head

to-matoes!

IF YOU WERE A SPINNING MASS OF WATER, YOU'D BE A

i think weed
go well together

IF YOU WERE
A NEWSPAPER
YOU WOULD BE

THE WALL *SWEET* JOURNAL

if you were
a president
you would be
Babe-raham Lincoln.

I
LOVE
YOU
BERRY
MUCH!

CAN YOU CLOSE THE BOOK NOW?

About
LoveBook®

We are a group of individuals who want to spread love in all its forms. We believe love fuels the world and every relationship is important. We hope this book helps build on that belief.

www.ingramcontent.com/pod-product-compliance
Lightning Source LLC
Chambersburg PA
CBHW041313110526
44591CB00022B/2896